Acknowledgments

Project Development Coordinator: **Kobus Reyneke**

Cover design and typography: **s.w.artz, inc.**

Editorial: **Ellen Fischbein**

Contributors: **Matthew and Tatiana Enochs,
Mike and Lynn Ryan,
Mary Jane Burns, Sue O'Brien,
Marvin and Paula Bernstein,
Eric and Kathy Lehmann,
Tom Lehmann, Jeff Kreismer,
Ben Polish, Eddie Charshafian,
Barbara Mitchell, Lori Walsh,
Rich Diamond and many others**

INTRODUCTION

A slice of life as American as apple pie …

Ranging from purple mountain's majesty to the depths of the Grand Canyon, *1776 Things to Love About America* is an affectionate portrait in words of our great land from sea to shining sea.

No single book could completely capture the diverse tapestry that is America. As "The Great Melting Pot," our heritage is drawn from lands around the world. We hope this volume serves as a reminder of some of those bits of Americana, both great and small, which bless our culture with unparalleled richness and our nation with incomparable vitality.

1776 THINGS TO LOVE ABOUT AMERICA

A Star-Spangled Salute to the USA

1776 THINGS TO LOVE ABOUT AMERICA

Mom ... Apple pie ... Fourth of July fireworks ... Mickey Mantle slamming a homer ...

Pike's Peak ... Erector Sets ... George M. Cohan ... Miss Piggy ... The Twist ... NASCAR ...

NASA ... "The Right Stuff" ... John Glenn ... "Life" magazine ... Alfred E. Neuman ...

Radio Flyer wagons ... Hershey bars ... Line dancing ... Clara Peller's "Where's the beef?" ...

Whistler's Mother ... Grandma Moses ... Raggedy Ann and Andy ... Washington Monument ...

**The Washington Monument excluded, no building
is allowed to be taller than 13 stories in our
nation's capital. You probably know why.**

A Star-Spangled Salute to the USA

George Washington Carver ... Washington State apples ... Georgia peaches ...

Jersey tomatoes ... Idaho potatoes ... Florida oranges ... White Castle burgers ...

Chicago's St. Patrick's Day Parade ... Spring training ..."Lassie" ... "Flipper" ... "Gentle Ben" ...

"Rin Tin Tin" ... Yogi Berra ... Scott Joplin ... March of Dimes ... IHOP ...

"Sing Along With Mitch" ... Olympic Peninsula ... Doris Day and Rock Hudson ...

**The reds win, 7 to 6,
in the stripes contest on Old Glory.**

1776 THINGS TO LOVE ABOUT AMERICA

Skateboards ... Roller Derby ... Full-service gas stations ... Pizza deliveries ...

Britney Spears ... "I Like Ike" buttons ... Nielsen ratings ...

Andy Williams' "Hawaiian Wedding Song" ... Sunset on the Grand Canyon ...

The Indianapolis 500 ... Jimmy Durante's "Goodnight Mrs. Calabash, wherever you are." ...

Rhett Butler and Scarlet O'Hara ... Miss Scarlet in the library with Clue ... Monopoly ...

The average U.S. coin circulates for 15 to 20 years while the life span of a dollar bill is approximately 18 months.

A Star-Spangled Salute to the USA

Scrabble ... Chutes and Ladders ... Yahtzee... "Its fun, it's easy, let's all play Parcheesi" ...

Garage sales ... "Doonesbury" ... Betty Crocker ... Mrs. Butterworth ... Aunt Jemima ...

Mr. Potato Head ... The All-American Soapbox Derby ... ESPN ... "Nickelodeon" ...

"Nick at Night" ... Columbus Day ... Woody Woodpecker ... PBS pledge drives ...

Jackie Robinson ... Little League ... Hickory Farms ... Car hop service ... Wurlitzer juke boxes ...

**"America is not merely a nation,
but a nation of nations."**

-President Lyndon B. Johnson

1776 THINGS TO LOVE ABOUT AMERICA

HBO ... The Rockettes ... Boogie boarding ... Howdy Doody time ... Walter Cronkite ...

Christmas tree at Rockefeller Center ... Pandas at the National Zoo ... Burma shave signs ...

Mayor Rudolph Giuliani ... The Arizona memorial ... Mickey Mouse ... Donald Duck ...

Uncle Scrooge ... "You've Got Mail" ... Sparky Anderson ...

Fritos, Cheetos and Doritos ... Disneyland ... Captain Kangaroo ...

**Does 1 Cherry Street ring a bell?
It was the New York City presidential address
of George Washington.**

A Star-Spangled Salute to the USA

Elvis Presley's "Jailhouse Rock" ... Swap meets ... The scent of newly mowed grass ...

The Petrified Forest ... "The Six Million Dollar Man" ... "The Bionic Woman" ...

Willie Nelson ... The City of Brotherly Love ... Instant messaging ...

Doubleheaders ... Joe DiMaggio ... John Wayne movies ... Music City, USA ...

The New York Public Library ... Buster Keaton movies ...

**The only mobile U.S. monuments
are San Francisco's cable cars.**

1776 THINGS TO LOVE ABOUT AMERICA

Ronco's Veg-O-Matic—"It slices, it dices, it juliennes potatoes!" ...

Surfing ... Barber poles ... The Good Humor man ... Bikinis ...

Outlet malls ... Puget Sound ... Wyatt Earp ... Video arcades ...

Penny arcades ... Lunch counters ... Old Packards ... Sea World ...

"Road" movies with Bing and Bob ... "Grease" ... Redwood groves ...

"Americans are like a rich father who wishes he knew how to give his son the hardships that made him rich."

-Robert Frost

The Colonel's secret recipe of eleven herbs and spices ... Soupy Sales ...

"The Huntley-Brinkley Report" ... Dick Butkus ... Drive-in theaters ... Drive-thru banks ...

Fast food drive-thru windows ... mint juleps ... Harlem's Apollo Theatre ...

Bugs Bunny's "Whats up Doc?" ... The Mamas and Papas ... 'Coonskin caps ...

Crazy Eights ... Tracy and Hepburn ... Superman and Batman ...

**Cartoonist Thomas Nast is credited with creating
the modern version of Santa Claus. He also created
the donkey for the Democratic Party and
the elephant for the Republicans.**

1776 THINGS TO LOVE ABOUT AMERICA

High school marching bands ... Tiger Woods ... Hoagies ... Subs ... Grinders ... Heros ...

Philly cheese steak ... Saturday morning cartoons ... Oreos ... Boston Marathon ... 4-H Clubs ...

Tilt-a-Whirl ... GI Joe action figures ... Mood rings ... Pinball machines ... Old Maid ...

The 76 trombones of "The Music Man" ... Big Bird ... Gallagher concerts ... Levis ...

Herman Melville's "Moby Dick" ... The Model T ... Polaroid cameras ... MTV ... Kickball ...

**It's a U.S. law that Yankee bean soup
must be served in the Congressional dining room
at all times.**

A Star-Spangled Salute to the USA

Shenandoah Valley ... TV dinners ... Teflon ... Michael Jordan ... Pop-Tarts ... Fort McHenry ...

"Teenage Mutant Ninja Turtles" ... Tony Bennett's "I Left My Heart In San Francisco" ...

Split-level house ... Apollo 13 ... Oscar the Grouch ... Freeze tag ...

Bobby sox ... The Jitterbug ... The Mashed Potato ... The Swim ... The Watusi ...

The Monkey ... The Jerk ... The Frug ... Wiffle ball ... The Super Ball ... Mario Brothers ...

Ruth Wakefield invented chocolate chip cookies in 1933.

1776 THINGS TO LOVE ABOUT AMERICA

Dallas Cowboys cheerleaders ... Mr. Whipple ... "Who's on First?" ...

Star Trek conventions ... Trekkies and Trekkers ... Mr. Spock's ears ...

"Dr. Spock's Baby and Child Care" ... The Preakness, Belmont Stakes and Kentucky Derby ...

"Barney Miller" ... Baseball cards in bike spokes ... Letters from Ed McMahon ... Bic Pens ...

Drivers Ed ... Thighmaster ... Nabisco ... Sergeant York ... Hank Williams (Sr. & Jr.) ...

The acronym GI stands for Government Issue.

A Star-Spangled Salute to the USA

Tinseltown ... Beantown ... Motown ... R&B ... The Vietnam Veterans Memorial ...

Street corner Doo-Wop ... Rock 'n' Roll ... Casey Stengel ... Shoeless Joe Jackson ...

Connie Mack ... Lou Gehrig ... Abner Doubleday ... Baseball Hall of Fame at Cooperstown ...

Dixieland Jazz ... American Legion halls ... Daughters of the American Revolution ... Bellbottoms ...

Bing Crosby's "White Christmas" ... Tina Turner ... Dial-A-Prayer ... Dial-A-Joke ...

**Eagles is the most popular name
for U.S. high school sports teams.**

1776 THINGS TO LOVE ABOUT AMERICA

Dennis Miller's rants ... "Broadway" Joe Namath ... "Battle Bots" ...

The Budweiser Clydesdales ... The Budweiser Frogs ... Kleenex ...

Kate Smith singing "God Bless America" ... Tony Hawk ... Beatles on "Ed Sullivan" ...

The Platters' "Twilight Time" ... "The Flying Nun" ... "The Monster Mash" ...

Quilting bees ... Spelling bees ... Aunt Bea ... Barney Fife ... Mayberry ... Red Barber ...

**The reason old American schoolhouses
were painted red is elementary.
It's simply because red was the cheapest paint available.**

A Star-Spangled Salute to the USA

Curt Gowdy ... Vin Scully ... Chris Schenkel ... Harry Caray ... Mel Allen ... Muhammad Ali ...

Joe Frazier ... Rocky Marciano ... The National Guard ... Jiffy Pop ... Fizzies ... Captain Crunch ...

Air shows on Armed Forces Day ... Slurpees at 7-11 ... 7-Up, the Uncola ... "Drink Canada Dry" ...

"Things go better with Coke" ... "Come Alive! You're in the Pepsi Generation" ...

"Wouldn't you like to be a Pepper too?"... Tailgate parties ... Direct TV ... Colorado River rapids ...

"Ask not what your country can do for you.
Ask what you can do for your country."

-President John F. Kennedy

1776 THINGS TO LOVE ABOUT AMERICA

Ethel Merman's "Everything's Coming Up Roses" ... Making S'mores on the campfire ...

Macaroni and cheese ... Firefighters ... The Smithsonian ... Johnson Space Center ...

SUVs ... Blue Light specials ... Raising the flag at Iwo Jima ... Steve Allen ...

Stevie Wonder ... Steven Wright ... Cindy Crawford ... "Oklahoma!" ... Hay rides ...

Seattle's Space Needle ... Carter's Little Liver Pills ... The Galloping Ghost ... Spuds McKenzie ...

**Twinkies was originally called
"Little Short-Cake Fingers."**

The Galloping Gourmet ... "The Partridge Family" ... Christopher Reeve ... Jim Thorpe ...

Taffy pulls ... Elliot Ness ... Hostess Twinkies ... Peter, Paul and Mary ... "The GE College Bowl" ...

Roller disco ... "The Longest Day" ... The Hokey-Pokey ... The Energizer Bunny ...

Nerf Ball ... Sequoia National Park ... Billy Beer ... John Elway... IBM ... Xerox ... Kinkos ...

FedEx ... UPS ... "I Love Lucy" ... The Arizona Meteor Crater ... Fred Flintstone ... Valley girls ...

**The first of the Barbie dolls
was launched in the U.S. in 1959
dressed in a zebra-style swimsuit.**

1776 THINGS TO LOVE ABOUT AMERICA

"The Dukes of Hazzard" ... Street musicians ... "Tammy" and "Gidget" flicks ... Fanny Brice ...

Honky-tonk piano ... Sam Snead ... Victory gardens ... Madison Square Garden ...

The Manhattan Project ... Bacon and eggs ... Simon and Garfunkel ... California Gold Rush ...

Satchel Paige ... James A. Michener ... Purina Dog Chow ... Calvin Klein ...

The Amazing Kreskin ... Freedom Trail ... "M*A*S*H" ... Pajama parties ... Freedom ...

"The British are coming, the British are coming."
-Paul Revere

A Star-Spangled Salute to the USA

Cruise control ... Barbecues ... Jackie O ... Fried green tomatoes ... Vince Lombardi ...

Volleyball ... "The Mickey Mouse Club" ... Cole Porter's "Night and Day" ... Ovaltine ...

Tomb of the Unknown Soldier ... Carolers at Christmastime ... "Wheel of Fortune" ...

The Cy Young Award ... Greyhound bus ... Don McLean's "American Pie" ... Indian head pennies ...

Tang ... PDQ ... Mom & Pop stores ... "Hello Dolly" ... The Sears Tower ... The Sears catalogue ...

There are 119 ridges around a quarter,
118 around a dime.

1776 THINGS TO LOVE ABOUT AMERICA

LL Bean ... Bean bags ... Block parties ... Sasquatch ... The Shadow knows ...

Boeing 727 ... Railroad engineers ... The Three Stooges ... Vanity license plates ... M&Ms ...

Butterfingers ... Tootsie Rolls ... Lifesavers ... Charms ... Goobers ... Raisinettes ... Mr. Goodbar ...

Mounds ... Almond Joy ... Clark Bar ... Losing a filling to a Milk Dud ... Milky Way ...

Reese's Peanut Butter Cups ... Snickers ... Jerry Rice ... Carl Sagan ... "Goosebumps" ...

Garnet Carter made a tiny name for himself when he invented miniature golf in Tennessee in 1927.

A Star-Spangled Salute to the USA

Grecian Formula ... "The Producers" ... Alan Shepard playing golf on the moon ... Will Rogers ...

John Kennedy ... John Henry ... John Hancock ... John Adams ... John D. Rockefeller ...

Johnny Appleseed ... "Heeere's Johnny" ... California's Napa Valley ... Brooklyn Dodgers ...

"A little dab'll do ya" ... Ritz crackers ... Speedy Alka-Seltzer ... Spring break ... Wilt the Stilt ...

Graffiti in subway stations ... The Policeman's Ball ... Independence Hall ...

According to the Boat Owners Association of the U.S., the most popular name given to vessels is Odyssey.

1776 THINGS TO LOVE ABOUT AMERICA

The Liberty Bell ... Oliver Wendell Holmes ... Times Square ... "Hee Haw" ...

The Sunday "New York Times" crossword puzzle ... Birdwatching ... Columbia River ...

Buffalo Bill Cody's Wild West Show ... Thundering herds of buffalo ... Woody Herman ...

Benny Goodman ... Tommy and Jimmy Dorsey ... Bagels and lox ... Silly Putty ... Telstar ...

Foghorn Leghorn ... Mario Lanza ... Jeans with a "scosh" more room ... Leisure suits ...

**Kansas City Chiefs owner Lamar Hunt
coined the term "Super Bowl."**

A Star-Spangled Salute to the USA

The U.S. Olympic Team ... "The A-Team" ... Paperboys ... Casper the Friendly Ghost ...

"Urban Cowboy" ... Gilly's ... Dude ranches ... Summer camp ... National Public Radio ...

"National Lampoon" ... "National Geographic" ... "USA Today" ... "The Hardy Boys" ...

"Nancy Drew" ... Cops at the local Dunkin' Donuts ... "The Wall Street Journal" ...

Family Reunions ... Donny and Marie Osmond ... Fuzzy dice ... Casey Kasem ... Sno-globes ...

"Patriotism is easy to understand in America. It means looking out for yourself by looking out for your country."

-President Calvin Coolidge

1776 THINGS TO LOVE ABOUT AMERICA

Purple Heart ... Congressional Medal of Honor ... Team Mascots ... Troll dolls ...

Remote controls ... Tuna casserole ... The Carpenters ... Dockers ... Old Faithful ...

"The Beverly Hillbillies" ... "Beverly Hills 90210" ... Beverly Sills ... The Metropolitan Opera ...

The Grand Ole Opry ... Patsy Cline ... Muzak ... Rodeo clowns ... Badlands National Park ...

"Rudolph the Red-Nosed Reindeer" ... Jean Shepard's "A Christmas Story" ... Bogie and Bacall ...

**Martin Van Buren was the first
U.S. born citizen to become president.**

A Star-Spangled Salute to the USA

Nick and Nora Charles ... "America's Funniest Home Videos" ... Sam Houston ...

Annie Oakley ... P.T. Barnum ... Tom Thumb ... Ice Capades ... Holiday on Ice ... Miracle on Ice ...

Ralph Kramden and Ed Norton ... Eating a Nathan's hot dog on Coney Island ...

Police scanners ... Dollywood ... Public access cable channels ... "Plastic or paper?" ...

Bibles in motel rooms ... "People" magazine ... "Meet the Press" ... The Salk polio vaccine ...

**Michael Jordan has appeared
on the cover of "Sports Illustrated"
more than anyone else.**

1776 THINGS TO LOVE ABOUT AMERICA

"Old Farmers Almanac" ... Pennsylvania Dutch country ... Covered bridges ... Hex signs on barns ...

Peter Falk's "Columbo" ... Montgomery Ward catalogue ... "Family Circle" cartoons ...

O. Henry ... Meals on Wheels ... ZZ Top ... Captain Midnight ... The Midnight Special ...

Wolfman Jack ... "American Graffiti" ... Whoopee cushions ... Rogers Hornsby ...

Ted Williams ... Willie Mays ... The Temptations' "My Girl" ... Amtrak ... The Gap ...

"America is a willingness of the heart."
-F. Scott Fitzgerald

A Star-Spangled Salute to the USA

Aerobics ... Hockey ... Richard Simmons ... Edgar Cayce ... Jimmy Doolittle and his Raiders ...

Duz detergent ... Mean Joe Greene ... Tom Landry ... Barbie and Ken ... The Big Apple ...

Mardi Gras in the Big Easy ... Big D ... "Beat The Clock" ... "Queen For A Day" ...

"Truth or Consequences" ... "The Price Is Right" ... "Password" ... "The Match Game" ...

Daytona International Speedway ... Dale Earnhardt ... Darrell Waltrip ... Mario Andretti ...

**The facial hair we call sideburns
got its name from a Civil War union general
who wore them, Ambrose Burnside.**

1776 THINGS TO LOVE ABOUT AMERICA

Richard Petty ... "Petticoat Junction" ... "Green Acres" ... Bob Dylan ... Neil Sedaka ... Neil

Diamond ... Neil Armstrong ... "Jack Armstrong, All American Boy" ... Andy Hardy ...

Tommy Smothers' "Mom always liked you best." ... Catalina Island ... Pet rocks ...

Phone cards ... General Douglas MacArthur ... Steak sauce ... Show and Tell ...

Peanut butter and jelly sandwiches ... Rock, paper, scissors and Odds & Evens ... Ant farms ...

Swanson introduced TV dinners to America in 1954.

A Star-Spangled Salute to the USA

Dungeons and Dragons ... YMCA and YWCA ... "Hallmark Hall of Fame" ... Pete Sampras ...

Golden Gate Bridge ... Dr. J ... Nancy Kerrigan ... Regis Philbin's "Is that your final answer?" ...

"Vanity Fair" ... "Collier's" ... "Harper's Bazaar" ... Frank Sinatra's "Strangers In The Night" ...

Dilbert ... Girl Scout cookies ... Hotwheels ... Garage bands ... Battle of the Bands ...

"Battle of the Network Stars" ... "American Gladiators" ... "Survivor" ... Hawaiian Islands ...

**Andrew Jackson was the only person
to serve in both the American Revolution
and the War of 1812.**

1776 THINGS TO LOVE ABOUT AMERICA

"Gilligan's Island" ... The American eagle ... Phil Spector's "Wall of Sound" ... Bozo the Clown ...

The Home Shopping Network ... QVC ... Emmett Kelly ... Red Skelton's "May God bless." ...

The Great American Smokeout ... Gameboy ... Jogging to the beat of your Walkman ...

Wall-to-wall shag carpeting ... Lava lamps ... "TV Guide" ... Microwave popcorn ...

Caramel corn ... Candy apples ... Corn dogs ... Pinky and the Brain ... Siskel and Ebert ...

The most landed upon space in Monopoly is Illinois Avenue.

A Star-Spangled Salute to the USA

The Roadrunner and Wiley E. Coyote ... Sundance Film Festival ... Kmart & Target ...

Battle re-enactments ... Miss Manners ... Buffalo nickel ... Devils Tower National Monument ...

Shrimp boats trolling Mobile Bay ... Tom Hanks ... Tom Cruise ... "Anchors Aweigh" ...

Dobie Gillis and Maynard G. Krebs ... Uncle Sam "I Want You" posters ... "The Marine Hymn" ...

The Army—"Be all you can be" ... "Join the Navy and see the world" ...

"We would rather die on our feet than live on our knees."

-President Franklin D. Roosevelt

1776 THINGS TO LOVE ABOUT AMERICA

"The few, the proud, the Marines" ... The Air Force's "Aim High" ... "This Is the Army" ...

"Off We Go Into the Wild Blue Yonder" ... "As the Caissons Go Rolling Along" ...

"The Battle Hymn of the Republic" ... "Dixie" ... Sloppy Joes ... Pigs in a Blanket ...

Weight Watchers ... Bally Total Fitness ... Gold's Gym ... The Brown Bomber ... Dave Barry ...

Lewis Grizzard ... Erma Bombeck ... Art Buchwald ... Robert Benchley ... James Thurber ...

**Lou Gehrig's baseball uniform number 4
was the first one retired in baseball history.**

The Algonquin Round Table ... Zorro ... Alaskan pipeline ... "Northern Exposure" ...

The Iditarod ... "Land of the Midnight Sun" ... Appalachian Trail ... The High Sierra ...

Donner Pass ... Lake Tahoe ... The Comstock Lode ... Carson City Mint ... Jessie Owens ...

The Monterey Bay Aquarium ... Clarence Birdseye ... Birthday parties at Chuck E. Cheese's ...

Moviephone ... Jack Nicholson ..."Old Yeller" ... "The Absent-Minded Professor" ... "Pollyanna" ...

President James Garfield's dog was named Veto.

1776 THINGS TO LOVE ABOUT AMERICA

Tinkerbell ... Office Christmas parties ... Water cooler gossip ... Casual Fridays ...

"It's a Wonderful Life" ... "Miracle on 34th Street" ... "Home Alone" ... "Holiday Inn" ...

"How the Grinch Stole Christmas" ... Al Jolson ... Currier & Ives ...

Norman Rockwell ... Bob Hope entertaining the troops ... John Paul Jones ... Admiral Byrd ...

Commodore Perry ... Perry Mason ... Mason jars ... Strawberry preserves ... County fairs ...

**"I venture to suggest that patriotism is not a short
and frenzied outburst of emotion
but the tranquil and steady dedication of a lifetime."**

-Adlai E. Stevenson

Blue ribbons ... Pie-eating contest ... Three-legged race ... Potato sack race ... Cookoffs ...

Hoedowns ... "Turkey in the Straw" ... Square dance caller ... The Mayflower ...

Nichols and May ... Stiller and Meara ... The button-down mind of Bob Newhart ...

Jim Carrey ... Drew Carey ... Pat Paulsen ... Frank Gorshin ... Donna Reed ... Rich Little ...

Little Debbie Snack Cakes ... "Little Women" ... Horn of Plenty ... "Honk If You Love ..." bumper stickers ...

Thomas Edison proposed to his wife in Morse code.
He began to lose his hearing at an early age,
so he taught his wife how to use Morse code.
She responded "Yes," also in Morse.

1776 THINGS TO LOVE ABOUT AMERICA

Craftsman tools … Husky tools … Whoopi Goldberg … Marty Robbins …

Eddy Arnold … Sitting Bull … Geronimo … Conway Twitty … Buck Owens … Buck Rogers …

Flash Gordon … Matchbox cars … The house that Ruth built … Cafe latte at Starbucks …

Water towers proudly proclaiming town names … JC Penney catalogues …

A Nor'easter blowing into Rockport … The Weather Channel … "Antiques Roadshow"…

"Time" magazine's first "Man of the Year"
was Charles Lindbergh in 1927.

A Star-Spangled Salute to the USA

The Beat Generation ... The Baby Boomers ... Generation X ... The Greatest Generation ...

Carnival midways ... Easter baskets ... Easter egg hunt ... The Easter Bunny ... Jelly beans ...

"Plop, plop, fizz, fizz" ... The Stork Club ... 21 ... Rainbow Room ... Four Seasons ...

The Copacabana ... Studio 54 ... Jordache jeans ... Ralph Lauren ... Gloria Vanderbilt ...

Martha Stewart ... "This Old House" ... Ken Griffey Jr. ...

**The U.S. flag, put on the moon on July 20, 1969,
was made of metal to withstand rock and dust debris.**

1776 THINGS TO LOVE ABOUT AMERICA

Garrison Keillor's "A Prairie Home Companion" ... Tom Bodett's "We'll leave the light on for ya." ...

"The Waltons" ... Sam Walton and Wal-Mart ... "Cheers" ... "Frazier" ... "Taxi" ... Cab Calloway ...

Duke Ellington ... Ella Fitzgerald ... Billie Holiday ... Count Basie ... Satchmo ... The Jazz Age ...

Bourbon Street ... "St. Louis Blues" ... St. Louis arch ... Smokey the Bear ...

James Brown, the hardest working man in show business ... Nehi Grape ... Frosty root beer ...

More phone calls are placed on Mother's Day
than on any other day in the U.S.
More collect calls are made on Father's Day
than any other day in our country.

A Star-Spangled Salute to the USA

AARP ... Bob Cousy ... Don Shula ... Bruce Brown's "Endless Summer" ... Betty Boop ...

Olive Oyl ... Blondie and Dagwood ... Rosie the Riveter ... "Entertainment Tonight" ...

"The Oprah Winfrey Show" ... Rosie O'Donnell ... Phil Donahue ... Mike Douglas ...

Merv Griffin and Arthur Treacher ... Dick Cavett ... Jack Paar ...

Sandra Day O'Connor ... Creamsicles ... Fudgesicles ... Popsicles ...

**"Liberty, when it begins to take root,
is a plant of rapid growth."**

-President George Washington

1776 THINGS TO LOVE ABOUT AMERICA

Henry Ford Museum & Greenfield Village ... Walt Whitman ... Scrapple ...

A soft pretzel with mustard ... Philadelphia Art Museum ... Reebok ... Earth Day ... Arbor Day ...

Memorial Day ... Labor Day ... Veterans Day ... "The McNeil-Lehrer Report" ... "60 Minutes" ...

Magic, Shaq and Kobe ... "Murder She Wrote" ... "Magnum P.I." ...

"Miami Vice" ... "Simon & Simon" ... Alvin, Simon and Theodore ... Dumbo ... Vidalia onions ...

**Do you know the faces of Gutzon Borglum?
Sure you do ... he's the artist who carved
Mount Rushmore.**

A Star-Spangled Salute to the USA

Chia Pets ... New York cheesecake ... New York strip steak ... Philadelphia cream cheese ...

Vermont maple syrup ... Wisconsin cheese ... Atlantic City Boardwalk ... Steel Pier ...

Santa Monica Pier ... Santa Monica Blvd ... Sunset Blvd ... The social satire of George Carlin ...

Improv sketch comedy from The Groundlings ... Second City ...

Steve Martin's "Well excuuuuse me." ... Shirley Temple ... The Goodyear Blimp ...

Alfred Mosher Butts invented the game of Lexico in 1946. Two years later Selchow & Righter bought the rights to it and changed the name to Scrabble.

1776 THINGS TO LOVE ABOUT AMERICA

Rummage sales ... Penny auctions ... Cruise through Alaska's inside passage ... Fresca ...

Crystal Light ... Dreamcatchers ... Lake Erie ... Honest Abe ... Colin Powell ...

Arlington National Cemetery ... Schwab's Drug Store ... The Brown Derby ...

Mann's Chinese Theater ... Sunset and Vine ... The Hollywood sign ...

Catching fireflies on a summer evening ... Treehouses with "No Girls Allowed" signs ...

"There can be no greater good than the quest for peace, and no finer purpose than the preservation of freedom."

-President Ronald Reagan

A Star-Spangled Salute to the USA

Koosh Balls ... Inaugural balls ... Ticker tape parades ... Ice cream parlors ...

Luncheonettes ... Automats ... "Life's a Beach" T-shirts ... Seminars in Hawaii ...

Conventions in Vegas ... Road trips ... The B&O Railroad ... Candy stripers ... Candy canes ...

Garlands ... Sidewalk Santas ... Church bells ... Welcome Wagon ...

The Oscar Meyer Weiner mobile ... Carnation Evaporated Milk ... Walter Payton ... PT 109 ...

**Andy Johnson was a tailor who made his own clothes —
until he became President of the United States.**

1776 THINGS TO LOVE ABOUT AMERICA

Ma and Pa Kettle ... The Muppets ... Palisades Park ...

Kool Aid pitchers with faces drawn on them ... Disneys "Fantasia" ... Liberace ... Slim Jims ...

Quaker Oats ... Monster trucks ... Demolition derby ... Drag strips ... Tic Tac Toe ...

Louisville Sluggers ... Navy Seals ... Green Berets ... Rescue squads ... Bloomingdales ... Saks ...

Tiffany & Co ... Old time radio ... Little Orphan Annie ... Fred Allen ... "The Green Hornet" ...

**The first picture on a U.S. postage stamp
was that of Benjamin Franklin.**

A Star-Spangled Salute to the USA

Bob and Ray ... "Nothin' says lovin' like somethin' from the oven" ... Lawrence Welk ...

FAO Schwartz ... Felix the Cat ... Sylvester ... Tweety Bird ... Bowl haircuts ...

Reggie Jackson ... Pete Rose ... George Brett ... Stan Musial ... Taylor pork roll ...

"The Cat in the Hat" ... Carl Sandburg ... Robert Frost ... Henry David Thoreau ...

Terry Bradshaw ... Morris the Cat ... Billy Jean King - Bobby Riggs match ... Metrecal ...

**Paul Revere took his midnight ride
on a horse named Brown Beauty.**

1776 THINGS TO LOVE ABOUT AMERICA

Hellman's mayonnaise ... Adopt-A-Road ... ASPCA ... Native American pottery ...

Hershey Kisses ... "Alice's Restaurant" ... Trader Vic's ... "Gone With the Wind"... Jell-O molds ...

Electric garage door openers ... Kazoos ... "The Mary Tyler Moore Show" ...

"Murphy Brown" ... Hangman ... Pinky Lee ... The Staten Island ferry ... 3-D movies ...

The Clapper ... The Philadelphia Orchestra ... Neil Simon's "The Odd Couple" ...

**Jimmy Carter was the first
U.S. president born in a hospital.**

A Star-Spangled Salute to the USA

Prom night limousine ... New York cab drivers ... Long boarders, Short boarders and Sailboarders ...

"Dueling Banjos" ... Honeymoons in Niagara Falls ... MIT .... The Great Smoky Mountains ...

"Hair" ... The Duke ... The Chairman of the Board ... Prince ... The Boss ... The King ...

Soda jerks ... Gas jockeys ... Saturday matinees ... C.A.R.E. ... Grilled cheese ...

Lionel trains ... Lookout Mountain ... "Seventeen" ... Abercrombie & Fitch ...

"I only regret that I have but one life
to lose for my country."

-Nathan Hale

1776 THINGS TO LOVE ABOUT AMERICA

Welch's grape juice ... Iceberg lettuce ... Chicken and dumplings ... Hands Across America ...

RVs held together with souvenir stickers ... The Mighty Carson Art Players ... "Friends" ...

"Seinfeld" ... Bosco ... Crossing guards on the corner ... "Dean Martin Celebrity Roasts" ...

John Deere ... Grain silos ... Red barns ... Amber waves of grain ...

Roadside farm stands at harvest time ... Farm Aid ... Smith Brothers Cough Drops ...

The color red on the American flag stands for hardiness and valor; white symbolizes purity and innocence; and blue is for vigilance and perseverance.

A Star-Spangled Salute to the USA

Hot air balloon races ... Cottages with white picket fences ... Country crafts ... Church festivals ...

Funnel cake ... Bill Russell ... Larry Bird ... The Garden State ... Carlton the Doorman ...

Old Philco Silvertone radios ... Audie Murphy ... Jack-O-Lanterns ... Trick-or-treaters ...

Orson Welles' "War of the Worlds" radio broadcast ... Kindergarten ... RCA Victor ...

The Boston Pops ... Organic vegetables ... New Age shops ... Monkey in the Middle ...

The national game of Canada, lacrosse, was invented by American Indians.

1776 THINGS TO LOVE ABOUT AMERICA

The California Raisins ... Potato knish ... Duncan yo-yos ... Jump rope ...

Badminton ... Sidewalk sales ... Eddie Murphy ... Coffeehouses ... Jack Kerouac ... McDonald's ...

Teddy bears ... Wax lips ... West Point ... The U.S. Naval Academy at Annapolis ...

The U.S. Air Force Academy at Colorado Springs ... Parris Island ... Fleet Week in San Francisco ...

Snap, Crackle and Pop ... Breyers ice cream ... Sarsaparilla ... Birch beer ...

"The country's honor must be upheld at home and abroad."

-President Theodore Roosevelt

A Star-Spangled Salute to the USA

The Ivy League ... Rock climbing ... Parasailing ... Waterskiing ... P.F. Flyers ... Keds ...

Razor scooters ... Big Wheels ... The National Archives ... Uneeda biscuits ... Oyster crackers ...

Popeye ... Tommy Lasorda ... Roger Maris ... Ichabod Crane, the Headless Horseman ...

"The Devil and Daniel Webster" ... "The Midnight Ride of Paul Revere"... "Readers Digest" ...

Kodak cameras ... Knute Rockne ... The Gipper ... Picnics ... Barney the Dinosaur ...

Yankee Noodle Dandy:
Thomas Jefferson introduced macaroni
to the United States ... and ice cream ... and waffles.

1776 THINGS TO LOVE ABOUT AMERICA

Patti Page ... Dinah Shore ... "See the USA in your Chevrolet" ... Hot tubs, Jacuzzis and spas ...

Manny, Moe and Jack, The Pep Boys ... Saratoga Springs ... Borscht belt ...

Sid Caesar and Imogene Coca ... Sharper Image ... The Keebler Elves ... Jolly Green Giant ...

Charlie the Tuna ... Bert and Harry Piels ... A sailboat regatta on Cape Cod Bay ...

E Pluribus Unum ... Tupperware parties ... Amelia Earhart ... Charles Lindbergh ...

**A King was once president of the United States.
When his parents divorced, Leslie King was adopted by
his stepfather and given a new name, Gerald Ford.**

A Star-Spangled Salute to the USA

Wiley Post ... The Bonneville Salt Flats ... Jackie Gleason's "One of these days, Alice" ...

Log Cabin maple syrup ... Steve and Eydie ... Wheaties ... Cheerios ... Sugar Frosted Flakes ...

Lavoris ... Monticello ... The Great Salt Lake ... The Mormon Tabernacle Choir ...

Glacier National Park ... "California Dreamin'" ... Oregon Trail ... Penn Station ...

MGM musicals ... Judy Garland's "Somewhere Over the Rainbow" ... Little Lulu ...

The largest amount of money in coins you could have without being able to make change for a dollar is $1.19 (three quarters, four dimes and four pennies).

1776 THINGS TO LOVE ABOUT AMERICA

Touch football … Tire swings and chestnut trees … The GI Bill … The Hard Rock Cafe …

Carl Lewis … Borden's Elsie the Cow … "Avon Calling" … Barbra Streisand … Jeff Foxworthy …

Gasoline Alley … Snuffy Smith … Beetle Bailey … Sunday brunch … "Bye Bye Birdie" …

The Kennedy compound at Hyannisport … Chuck Berry …

Frankie Valli and the Four Seasons … Fannie Farmer candy … "Ding-Dong School" … Hi-C …

Superman was born on February 29.

A Star-Spangled Salute to the USA

Rita Hayworth ... Ava Gardner ... Bette Davis ... Maine lobster ... Alaskan King crabs ...

Maryland soft-shell crabs ... Hawaiian pineapples ... Texas chili ... Boston baked beans ...

Manhattan clam chowder ... New England clam chowder ... The King Family ... Clearasil ...

Nature hikes ... Paintball games ... Laser tag ... "I don't get no respect." ... Paper airplanes ...

Model airplanes ... Pay toilets ... Toys For Tots ... Fruitcake ... Geraldo opening Capone's vault ...

"I shall know but one country. The ends I aim at shall be my country's, my God's, and Truth's. I was born an American; I will live an American; I shall die an American."

-Daniel Webster

1776 THINGS TO LOVE ABOUT AMERICA

Cleveland's Rock & Roll Hall of Fame ... Kennedy Center Awards ... The Oscars ...

The Emmys ... The Grammys ... The Tonys ... American Comedy Awards ...

The Country Music Awards ... The Police Athletic League ... Martin Luther King Jr. ...

Babe Didrikson Zaharias ... Dorothy Hamill ... Cathy Rigby ... Rock candy ... Rockabilly ...

"Rock of Ages" ... "The quicker picker-upper" ... Damon Runyon ... The AFL-CIO ... UAW ...

**Until Thomas Edison suggested using "Hello,"
most people answered their phones by saying "Ahoy."**

Shriners Hospitals ... St. Jude Hospital ... Doll hospitals ... The Wizard of Menlo Park ...

BVDs ... Westminster Kennel Club ... Mark Spitz ... Matt Helm ... "Yankee Magazine" ...

"Sports Illustrated" ... "Playbill" ... "Rugrats" ... Hayden Planetarium ... Kewpie dolls ...

Kathie Lee Gifford ... Frank Gifford ... Dandy Don Meredith ... Howard Cosell ...

"Monday Night Football" ... "Saturday Night Live" ... "Wayne's World" ... "Coneheads" ...

**He was born in England in 1903 and was once a boxer
who fought under the ring name Packy East.
This man went west and became one of America's most
beloved entertainers, Bob Hope.**

1776 THINGS TO LOVE ABOUT AMERICA

E.T. ... ALF ... SETI (Search for Extra-Terrestrial Intelligence) ...

MADD (Mothers Against Drunk Drivers) ... Augusta National Golf Course ... Izod ...

Pebble Beach ... Ray Charles ... "Georgia On My Mind" ...

Johnny Mathis and Barry White mood music ... The Lincoln Memorial ... "Citizen Kane" ...

LPs, 45s and 78s ... Sunoco ... Ajax ... April showers ... Jayne Mansfield ...

"America is not a mere body of traders; it is a body of free men.
Our greatness is built upon our freedom — is moral, not
material. We have a great ardor for gain;
but we have a deep passion for the rights of man."

-President Woodrow Wilson

A Star-Spangled Salute to the USA

Gene Kelly "Singing in the Rain" ... Wrigley gum ... Coleman camping gear ... Daniel Boone ...

Davy Crockett ... Jim Bowie ... Jim Croce ... Jimmy Dean ... Jimmie Foxx ... Fenway Park ...

Wrigley Field ... "Trix are for kids" ... Bit-O-Honey ... Turkish Taffy ... Pixie Sticks ... Twister ...

Yahoo ... Monster.com ... Bill Gates ... "Revenge of the Nerds" ... Extreme sports ...

Nat King Cole ... Coffee breaks ... Brown-bagging it ... Sammy Davis Jr. ...

**The only product named after the U.S. Patent Office
is patent leather, introduced in 1916.**

1776 THINGS TO LOVE ABOUT AMERICA

Cracker Barrel restaurants ... Mallomars ... Mixmaster mixers ... Doan's pills ... Pepto Bismol ...

School nurses ... Wild West ghost towns ... The Secret Service ... The FBI ...

The U.S. Coast Guard ... The Franklin Institute ... American Museum of Natural History ...

Waldorf salad ... Grant's Tomb ... New York Stock Exchange ... Cream of Wheat ...

Instant Postum ... Flintstone vitamins ... Ride-on mowers ... Table tennis ... Shuffleboard ...

**Presidents Thomas Jefferson and John Adams
died on the exact same day — the fourth of July, 1826.**

A Star-Spangled Salute to the USA

Hoagy Carmichael's "Stardust" ... Roaring Twenties ... Maxwell Smart and Agent 99 ...

"Entertainment Weekly" ... "Rolling Stone" ... "Billboard" ... "Variety" ...

Chocolate-covered pretzels ... CD burners ... Screen names ... Smart cards ... Boxcar Willie ...

Johnny Cash ... Waylon Jennings ...Yogi Bear ... The Lone Ranger ... Tonto ...

Jack London ..."Call of the Wild" ... Zane Grey ... Roasting marshmallows ...

Benjamin Franklin invented, among other things, bifocals, swim fins, the odometer and fire insurance.

1776 THINGS TO LOVE ABOUT AMERICA

Ernest Hemingway ... Serena & Venus Williams ... "Ozzie and Harriet" ... Mr. Green Jeans ...

High school yearbooks ... "Rocky" ... Tennis elbow ... Nintendo thumb ... Frisbee finger ...

The Victorian mansions of Newport ... Boston's Beacon Hill ... Scott Carpenter ...

Will Smith ... Sonny ...Cher... Chock Full O' Nuts ... Jack Dempsey ...

Evander Holyfield ... George Foreman ... Sunshine State ... Mighty Mouse ...

**The White House was once painted grey
and called the Executive Mansion.**

Bazooka bubble gum ... Wayne Newton ... "The Love Boat" ... The Jefferson Memorial ...

Bookmobiles ... Wolfgang Puck ... Veterans of Foreign Wars ... Voice of America ... Pac-Man ...

Skiing and Snow boarding ... Local Rotary Clubs ... Gatorade ... The "Show Me" state ...

Rodeos ... Lincoln's Gettysburg Address ... The Emancipation Proclamation ...

The Underground Railroad ... "Bowling For Dollars" ... Paul Harvey ... July 20, 1969 ...

"Unlike many other people less happy,
we give our devotion to a government,
to its Constitution, to its flag, and not to men."

-President Benjamin Harrison

1776 THINGS TO LOVE ABOUT AMERICA

June 14 ... Plymouth Rock ... Raking leaves on a crisp autumn afternoon ... Mr. Salty ...

Mattel ... Wham-O ... Kenner ... Diana Ross and the Supremes ... The Temptations ...

The Four Tops ... Old Ironsides ... Tomorrow Land ... Frontier Land ... Cinderella's Castle ...

Asheville's Biltmore Estate ... The Hearst Castle ... Peter Benchley's "Jaws" ...

800 numbers ... Wally Schirra ... Mini-skirts ... Platform shoes ... Hot pants ...

**The "D" in D-Day stands for "Day"
to reiterate its military importance.**

Admiral Chester Nimitz ... Bull Halsey ... "Tie a Yellow Ribbon 'Round the Old Oak Tree" ...

View Master ... Gypsy Rose Lee ... Sally Rand ... Tiger Stadium ... Ebbets Field ...

Dodger Stadium ... W.C. Fields ... Mae West ... Screwball comedies ... Woolworth's 5&10 ...

Whale watching ... Shoney's ... CB radios ... "Smokey and the Bandit" ... Cell phones ...

"American Gothic" ... The Polar Bear Club ... Tanning salons ... Saunas ... Shirley Jones ...

In 1911, a West Point applicant flunked his physical, so the military school granted admission to the next candidate — future U.S. President Dwight D. Eisenhower.

1776 THINGS TO LOVE ABOUT AMERICA

Helen Hayes ... Mary Martin ... Wink Martindale ...

Bill Cullen, Allen Ludden and Gene Rayburn ... Zestfully clean ... Joe Izusu ... Tony the Tiger ...

Newman's Own pasta sauces ... Roy Orbison trilling "Only the Lonely" ... Ellis Island ...

Ramshackle waterfront bait shacks ... "Real People" ... The 1964 New York World's Fair ...

The Unisphere ... Archie and Edith Bunker ... Musical Chairs ...

"Those who expect to reap the blessings of freedom must, like men, undergo the fatigue of supporting it."

-Thomas Paine

A Star-Spangled Salute to the USA

America's Bi-Centennial celebrations ... "Saturday Night Fever" ... Ernie Kovacs ... Garry Moore ...

Milton Berle's "I'll kill you a million times!" ... Vaudeville ...

George Burns and Gracie Allen ... Billy Ray Cyrus' "Achy-Breaky Heart" ... Walt Kelly's "Pogo" ...

Father Flanagan's Boys Town ... Bed & Breakfasts in Mendocino, Cape May and Provincetown ...

Casey Jones ... Valley Forge ... Carlsbad Caverns ... "The Man from U.N.C.L.E." ...

Quick — What's the only state with a one-syllable name?
... Maine

1776 THINGS TO LOVE ABOUT AMERICA

Y.A. Tittle ... Rosey Grier ... Bubba Smith ... Pez dispensers ... Kermit the Frog ...

Discotheques ... Go-go boots ... Nehru jackets ... Ben and Jerry's ... Animal crackers ...

The Marx brothers ... "You Bet Your Life" ... "The $64,000 Question" ...

"Twenty-One" ... Mark McGwire and Sammy Sosa ... Woodward and Bernstein ...

Edgar Bergen and Charlie McCarthy ... Paul Winchell and Jerry Mahoney ...

Count 'em — There are 26 states named
on the back of a five-dollar bill.
(You'll need a magnifying glass for this one.)

Hide and Seek ... Piggy banks ... The Thousand Islands ...

Minnesota's Land of 10,000 Lakes ... Ham radios ... Hank Aaron ... Shirts against Skins ...

Charades ... Zion National Park ... Lenox china ... Spencer Gifts ... Purple mountain's majesty ...

Hush Puppies ... Buzz Lightyear and Woody ... Plastic soldiers ... Mr. Blackwell ...

"Hawaii Five-O" ... Good & Plenty ... Chuckles ... Dots ... Junior mints ... Jujyfruits ...

One of our national treasures, Elvis Presley, had a twin brother, Aaron, who died shortly after birth.

1776 THINGS TO LOVE ABOUT AMERICA

"Laugh-In" ... Dick Martin's "You bet your bippy" ... "Sock it to me" ...

The Fickle Finger of Fate ... Chris Evert ... Denny's ... Box kites ...

Minutemen ... "Hey, Culligan man" ... Gus Grissom ...

"Ted Mack's Original Amateur Hour" ... American Movie Classics ... Flagpole sitting ...

"The Hustle" ... John Denver's "Rocky Mountain High" ... Charles Atlas ... Jack LaLanne ...

**"I have a dream. I have a dream that one day,
on the red hills of Georgia, sons of former slaves and the
sons of former slaveowners will be able to sit down
at the table of brotherhood."**

-Martin Luther King Jr.

"98 Pound weakling" ... BLT sandwiches ... Bloodmobile ... "It's a Mad, Mad, Mad, Mad World" ...

Hamburger Helper ... Tinker-to-Evers-to-Chance ... Minute rice ... Instant mashed potatoes ...

Bumper pool ... Glenn Miller's "Moonlight Serenade" ... "Chattanooga Choo Choo" ...

Happy face buttons ... The U.S. Constitution ... Freshly-squeezed orange juice ...

The Tunnel of Love ... Bathing beauties ... The Ivory Soap baby ...

**The first president to live in the White House was
John Adams. When he and his wife moved in,
only six rooms were finished and Abigail
used to hang up her laundry in the East Room.**

1776 THINGS TO LOVE ABOUT AMERICA

Snapping towels in locker rooms ... The seventh inning stretch ... Designated hitter ...

Bleacher creatures ... Carvel Ice Cream store ... Brooklyn Bridge ... Mercury head dimes ...

Cabbage Patch dolls ... Rock 'em Sock 'em robots ... Hungry Hungry Hippo ...

Poinsettias ... Chain letters ... Doing the limbo at a pool party ... Electric can openers ...

Pocket harmonicas ... Declaration of Independence ... Air Stream trailers ... Delmonico's ...

**The distance between home plate and second base
on our national pastime's baseball diamond
is 127 feet 3 3/8".**

A Star-Spangled Salute to the USA

Lindy's ... Mama Leone's ... Miss America ... Flexible Flyer sleds ... Snow forts ...

Snowmen ... Snowballs in the freezer ... Pop guns ... Colorforms ...

Tiddlywinks ... Croquet ... Jimmy Stewart ... Henry Fonda ...

Gary Cooper ... James Cagney ... Marilyn Monroe ... The Monroe Doctrine ...

Manifest Destiny ... The Louisiana Purchase ... Monty Hall and "Let's Make A Deal" ...

"Give me liberty or give me death."
-Patrick Henry

1776 THINGS TO LOVE ABOUT AMERICA

Chuck Barris and "The Gong Show" ... Foosball ... Air hockey ... Air guitar ... Billy Joel ...

The Kingston Trio ... Hot rods ... Chris Craft cabin cruisers ... Ouija boards ...

Crater Lake, Oregon ... Buddy Holly and the Crickets ... Palm Pilots ... Candy necklaces ...

Necco Wafers ... Sugar Daddy ... Whoppers ... The Ziegfeld Follies ... Time-Life music ...

Jock rock stadium music ... Stress balls ... Fruit Loops ... Cal Ripken Jr. ...

**George Jung, a Los Angeles noodlemaker,
invented fortune cookies in 1916.**

A Star-Spangled Salute to the USA

Stuckey's nut logs ... "Kukla, Fran and Ollie" ... Shari Lewis and Lamb Chop ...

White Fang and Black Tooth ... Pillbox hats ... "A Chorus Line" ... "Mr. Ed" ... Break dancing ...

Isaac Asimov ... Ray Bradbury ... Robert Heinlein ...

Tom Brokaw, Peter Jennings, & Dan Rather ...

"Everything is Beautiful" by Ray Stevens ... Lake Champlain ... Edward R. Murrow ...

**The only letter not used in the spelling
of any of the 50 states in the U.S. is "q."**

1776 THINGS TO LOVE ABOUT AMERICA

Singing telegrams ... Letterman's Top Ten List ... The Campbell Kids ... Tarzan ...

"Fiddler On The Roof" ... "Casablanca" ... "Candid Camera" ... Candy Land ...

Soul Sister #1, Aretha Franklin ... Shelling on the beaches of Sanibel ... Jiminy Cricket ...

General "Stormin'" Norman Schwarzkopf ... "Casey at the Bat" ... "Nightline" ...

"ABC's Wide World Of Sports" ... Cesar Chavez ... The Heisman Trophy ... MVP awards ...

**It's 630 feet by 630 feet and is officially dubbed
"The Jefferson National Expansion Monument."
You know it better as the Gateway Arch in St. Louis.**

Super Bowl rings ... The Founding Fathers ... Howard Johnson's 28 Flavors ...

San Francisco Sourdough ... Hawaiian shirts ... Kentucky bluegrass ... Barry Bonds ...

"Shindig" ... "Hullabaloo" ... "Hootenanny" ... 50's sci-fi atomic mutation flicks ...

"Trick or treat for UNICEF" ... The American Red Cross ... The Salvation Army ...

Army-Navy Game ... The Sugar Bowl, Rose Bowl, Cotton Bowl and Orange Bowl ...

**Camp David, the presidential retreat, was called
Shangri-La until President Eisenhower
renamed it after his grandson in 1953.**

1776 THINGS TO LOVE ABOUT AMERICA

Orville and Wilbur at Kitty Hawk ... The Spirit of St. Louis ... Memphis Belle ...

P-51 Mustang ... '65 Mustang ... '56 T-Bird ... The Edsel ...

The '48 Tucker ... Yosemite ... "The Washington Post" ... Mississippi riverboats ...

"Maverick" ... Marshal Dillon and "Gunsmoke" ... "Bonanza" ... Malt shoppes ...

Banana splits ... The Ozarks ... The New York Marathon ...

"My affections were first for my own country,
and then, generally, for all mankind."

-Thomas Jefferson

The strength and grit of coal miners ... "March of the Wooden Soldiers" ...

"Remember the Maine!" ... The Fuller Brush man ... Helen Keller ... Chicken soup ...

"The Wizard of Oz" ... J. Fred Muggs ... The Dough Boys of WWI ...

The Pillsbury Dough Boy ... Minnesota Fats ... "Hollywood Squares" ...

Words and music by Irving Berlin ... Lighthouse keepers ... The Boston Tea Party ...

**Silent Cal Coolidge always lived up to his reputation.
A woman sat next to him at a dinner gathering and said,
"You must talk to me, Mr. Coolidge. I made a bet today
that I could get more than two words out of you."
The former U.S. president replied, "You lose."**

1776 THINGS TO LOVE ABOUT AMERICA

Habitat for Humanity ... The Bronx Zoo ... The San Diego Zoo ...

Dogs playing Frisbee ... The pursuit of happiness ...

Pittsburgh's Golden Triangle ... The Quad Cities ... The Upper Peninsula of Michigan ...

Cheese Whiz ... Religious freedom ... Slinky ... Tinker Toys ... Play-Doh ...

Golden Gloves boxing ... Mike Ditka ... " Refrigerator" Perry ... Johnny Unitas ...

**To patriots Paul Revere and Betsy Ross,
January 1st rang in the New Year in more ways than one.
It was also their birthday.**

A Star-Spangled Salute to the USA

Joe Montana ... Spiderman ... Marvel comics ... Perry Como ... Mayo Clinic ...

"On Top Of Old Smokey" ... Dr. Robert Goddard ... Albert Einstein ...

"Poor Richard's Almanac" ... Thomas Paine ... Pink lemonade ... OK Corral ...

The Peter Principle ... Murphy's Law ... Horatio Alger ... Esther Williams' movies and pools ...

Daffy Duck ... "The Carol Burnett Show" ... Mr. Peanut ... Fluffernutters ... Stanley Steamer ...

"Let every nation know, whether it wishes us well or ill, that we shall pay any price, bear any burden, meet any hardship, support any friend, oppose any foe to assure the survival and the success of liberty."

-President John F. Kennedy

1776 THINGS TO LOVE ABOUT AMERICA

One-hour optical stores ... Golden oldies stations ...

Texaco's "You can trust your car to the man who wears the star." ... Juice bars ...

Big Sky country ... "Hill Street Blues" ... Bill Moyers ...

Community colleges ... Graceland ... Mulder and Scully ... Zoot suits ...

Arnold Palmer ... Jack Nicklaus ... Oklahoma land rush ... Franklin D. Roosevelt ...

**Benjamin Franklin was the fifteenth child
of a Boston soapmaker.**

A Star-Spangled Salute to the USA

Mr. Magoo ... "Mary Hartman, Mary Hartman" ... "Fernwood 2night" ...

"Don't leave home without it." ... The Space Shuttle ... Lance Armstrong ...

Napping in a hammock ... Parker Brothers ... Milton Bradley ... Campfire girls ...

Big Brothers and Big Sisters ... Etch-A-Sketch ... Dollar stores ... Sandy Koufax ...

Tom Seaver ... Nolan Ryan ... Yoo-Hoo ... Eggnog ... Mistletoe ... Sleigh rides ...

Lake Michigan is the only one of the Great Lakes entirely in the U.S.

1776 THINGS TO LOVE ABOUT AMERICA

Sadie Hawkins Day ... Li'l Abner ... Tennessee Ernie Ford ... "From Here to Eternity" ...

Tumbleweeds, sagebrush and cactus ... Indian cliff dwellings ...

Sophie Tucker, the Last of the Red Hot Mamas ... Electric toothbrush ...

Pat Boone and his white bucks ... The Black Hills ... The Blue Angels ...

Branson, MO ... The Marshall Plan ..."Takes a licking and keeps on ticking" ...

**President Rutherford B. Hayes' wife
was nicknamed Lemonade Lucy
because she refused to serve alcohol in the White House.**

A Star-Spangled Salute to the USA

Scott Hamilton ... Brian Boitano ... Peggy Fleming ... Seward's Folly ... Humane Society ...

The Audubon Society ... The Sierra Club ... Greenpeace ... Hansom cabs ...

Front yard lemonade stands ... Infomercials ... Charlie Pride, Charlie Rich and Charlie Daniels ...

Church Bingo ... Fire Prevention Week ... Bathroom Reading Week ... Crash Test Dummies ...

McGruff, the Crime Dog ... The old swimmin' hole ... Nine-passenger station wagons ...

English muffins were first made in America.

1776 THINGS TO LOVE ABOUT AMERICA

Robin Williams on a roll … Front porch swing … Junkyard dogs … "Say it with flowers" …

The Nineteenth Hole … Flip Wilson's "The Devil made me do it." …

Locomotives, coal tenders and cabooses … The Pony Express …

"When it absolutely, positively has to be there overnight." … Key West's "Conch Republic" …

Surf fishing … Ice fishing … Rainbow trout … Franklin stoves … "Look for the union label" …

"I contend that the strongest of all governments is that which is most free."

-President William Henry Harrison

A Star-Spangled Salute to the USA

"Jingle Bell Rock" ... "Frosty the Snowman" ... "I'll Be Home For Christmas" ...

"Put a tiger in your tank." ... New England's cedar shingles and salt spray ... Foster Grants ...

Cliff's Notes ... Pin the Tail on the Donkey ... Tom Sawyer and Huck Finn ...

"California Girls" ... Coleslaw on paper plates ... Scotch plaid coolers filled with pop ...

Your kite caught in a tree ... Woodsy Owl ... The Fonz ...

When Francis Scott Key wrote the
"Star-Spangled Banner", the U.S. flag had fifteen stripes
representing the amount of states at that time.

1776 THINGS TO LOVE ABOUT AMERICA

Reciting "The Pledge of Allegiance" in school assembly ... The heady aroma of a New York deli ...

Chinese take-out ... Prince William Sound ... Spanky and Our Gang ...

Lewis and Clark ... Steven King ... Mary Higgins Clark ... Ellery Queen ...

Baseball cards, marbles and tops in old cigar boxes ... Harleys ... The office football pool ...

The Harlem Globetrotters ... Rodeo Drive ... Flea markets ...

You could say "Merry Christmas" and "Happy Birthday" on the same day to the founder of the American Red Cross, Clara Barton (born December 25, 1821) ... ditto for fellow Americans Humphrey Bogart, Barbara Mandrell, Sissy Spacek and Rickey Henderson.

A Star-Spangled Salute to the USA

Maytag repairman ... The Golden Spike ... Bruce Jenner ...

"Give me your tired, your poor, your huddled masses yearning to breathe free" ...

Food courts at the mall ... Boy Scouts ... Cub Scouts ... Brownies ...

Cape Hatteras Lighthouse ... Mount Rushmore ... Grizzly bears ... Concord and Lexington ...

The Battleship Missouri ... Thornton Wilder ... Ten-gallon hats ... "In God we trust" ...

"The course of this conflict (with terrorists) is not known, yet its outcome is certain. Freedom and fear, justice and cruelty, have always been at war, and we know that God is not neutral between them."

-President George W. Bush

1776 THINGS TO LOVE ABOUT AMERICA

The Teaberry Shuffle ... New York's Plaza Hotel ... Rosa Parks ... "Have Gun Will Travel" ...

"Oil, Black Gold, Texas Tea" ... Quilted bathroom tissue ... Joy buzzers ...

Lee Greenwood's "God Bless the USA" ... "Amazing Grace" and "Peace in the Valley" ...

Stephen Foster tunes ... Donating blood ... H.L. Mencken ... Frankie and Annette ...

Dick Clark ... Art Linkletter ... John Barrymore ... Gadfly Michael Moore ...

**Former astronaut John Glenn and baseball great
Ted Williams were co-pilots during
Korean War bombing missions.**

A Star-Spangled Salute to the USA

Lionel Hampton ... Ansel Adams ... Batting cages ... Driving ranges ...

Basketball hoops in the driveway ... Garth Brooks ... R2D2, C3PO and Chewbacca ...

The Hair Club for Men ... Silicon Valley ... Billy Graham ... Alexander Graham Bell ...

Mary Lou Retton ... Graham crackers ... Suzy Chapstick ... Thanksgiving ...

Turkey dinner with cranberry sauce and stuffing ... Pumpkin pie ... "Red River Valley" ...

White House ... Blue Ridge Mountains ... The Wabash Cannonball ... Varsity letter jackets ...

**According to Hoyle,
poker is the national card game of the U.S.**

1776 THINGS TO LOVE ABOUT AMERICA

Adirondack chairs ... Disney World ... Carnac the Magnificent ... Hula hoops ... Bowling leagues ...

Jerome Kern ... "Happy Days" ... Skeeball machines ... Grizzly Adams ... "Home on the Range" ...

Crackerjack ... "The New Yorker" ... Abigal Adams, Dolley Madison and Eleanor Roosevelt ...

South of the Border ... The scent of cocoa butter at the beach ... Sandlot softball games ...

The Statue of Liberty ... And Porky Pig's "Th-th-that's all, folks!"

How many more can you think of?

GOD BLESS AMERICA!